Hush, Little

Alien

Daniel Kirk

Hyperion Books for Children • New York

Hush, little alien,
don't say a word,

Papa's gonna catch
you a goonie bird.

If that goonie bird flies too far,

Papa's gonna lasso you a shooting star.

If that shooting star's too hot,

Papa's gonna

find you an

astronaut !

If that astronaut
should fight,
Papa's gonna bring
you a satellite!

If that
satellite
gets away,
Papa's gonna
take you to
the Milky Way!

If that milk
has got no cream,
papa's gonna
buy you a
laser beam!

If that laser makes things melt,

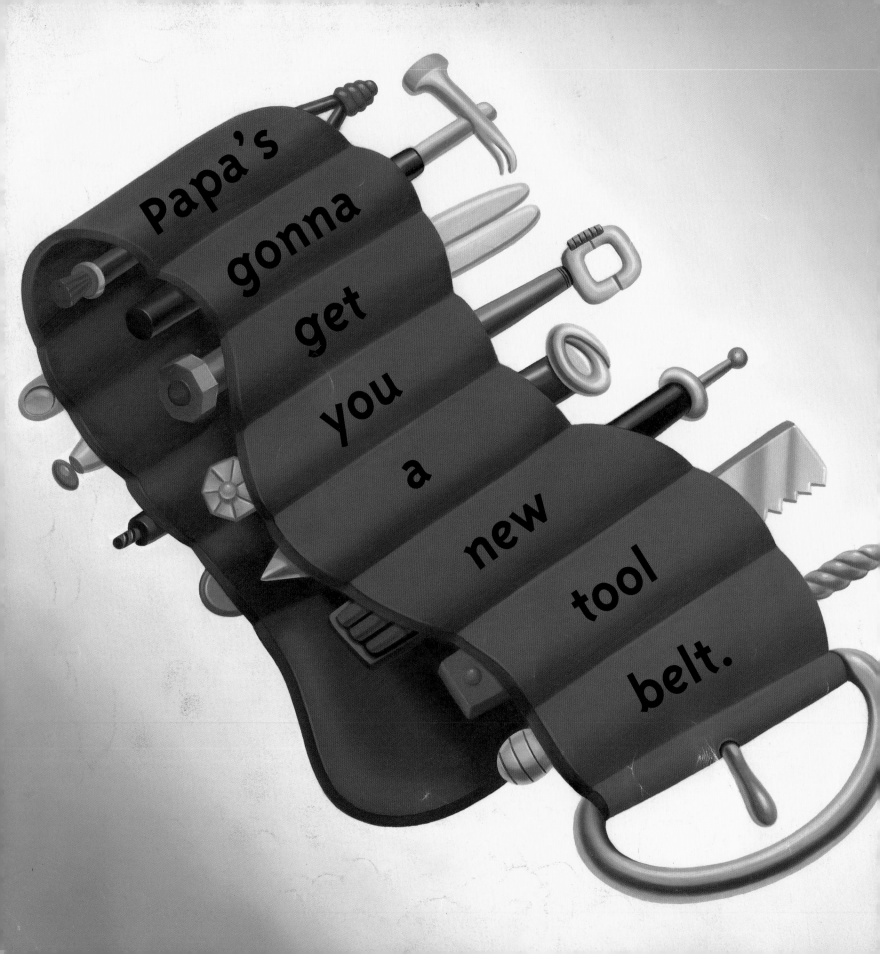

And
when
that
rocket
ship
takes
flight,

Papa's gonna give you
a kiss good night*!*

For Raleigh, the boy with his head in the stars

Text © 1999 by Daniel Kirk.
Illustrations © 1999 by Daniel Kirk.

Printed in Hong Kong by South China Printing Company Ltd.
First Edition
1 3 5 7 9 10 8 6 4 2

The illustrations in this book were created using
oil paint on gessoed Strathmore paper.
This book was set in Triplex 45pt.

Library of Congress Cataloging-in-Publication Data
Hush, little alien/by Daniel Kirk; illustrated by Daniel Kirk.
p. cm.
Summary: In this adaptation of the old lullaby, "Hush, Little Baby,"
an extraterrestrial child is promised an assortment of outer space presents
ending with a good night kiss from his adoring father.
ISBN 0-7868-0538-2—ISBN 0-7868-2469-7
1. Folk songs, English—Texts.
[1. Lullabies. 2. Folk songs.] I. Title.
PZ8.3.K6553Hu 1999   [782.42]—dc21 99-10651